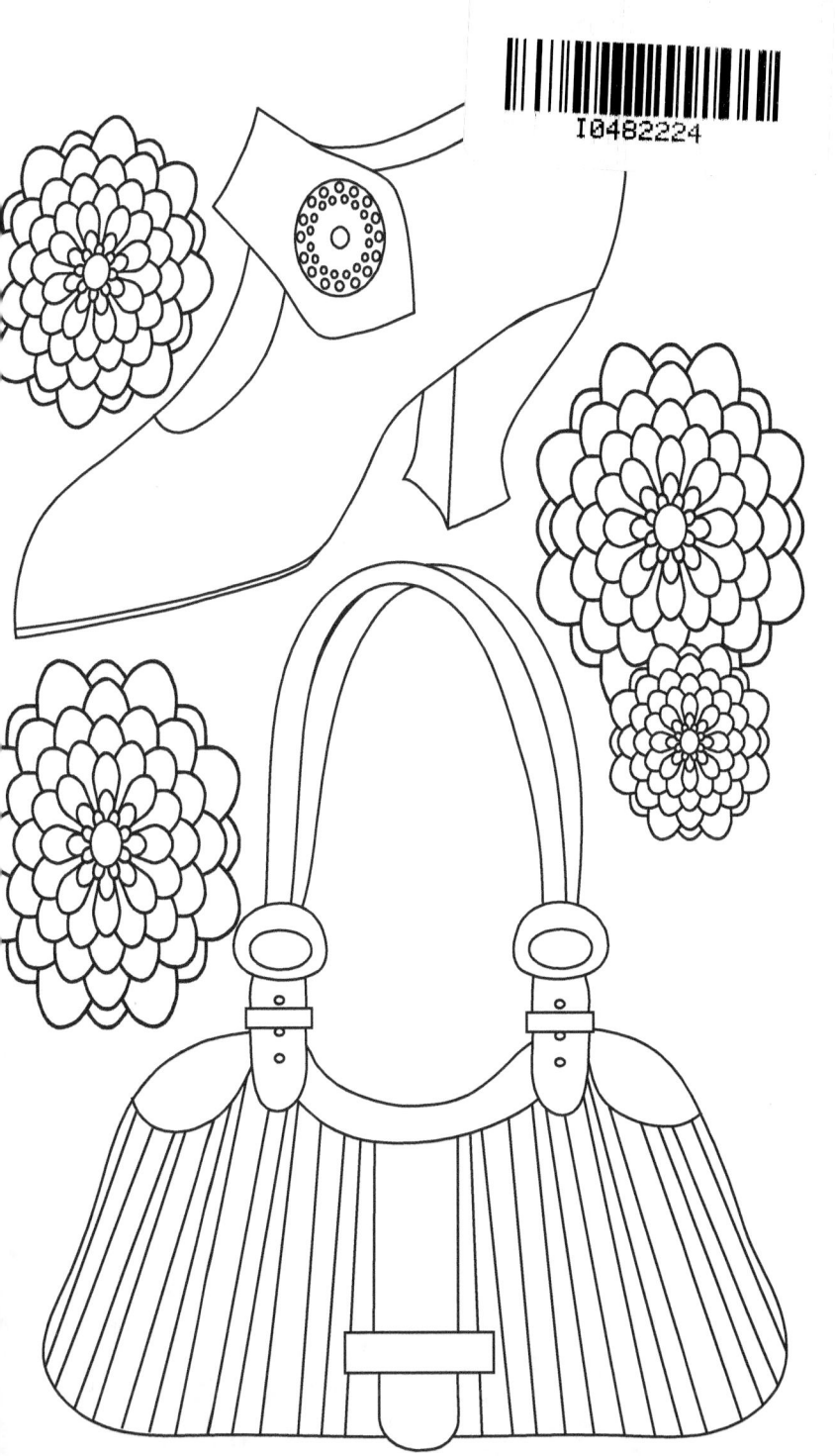

Vintage Handbags and Shoes

Travel Edition

ADULT COLORING BOOKS

By Beth Ingrias

Want to color
more for FREE?

Get a FREE 25 page adult coloring book

visit

www.BethIngrias.com

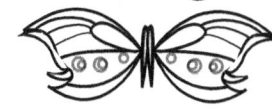

ISBN-13: 978-1533244246
ISBN-10: 1533244243

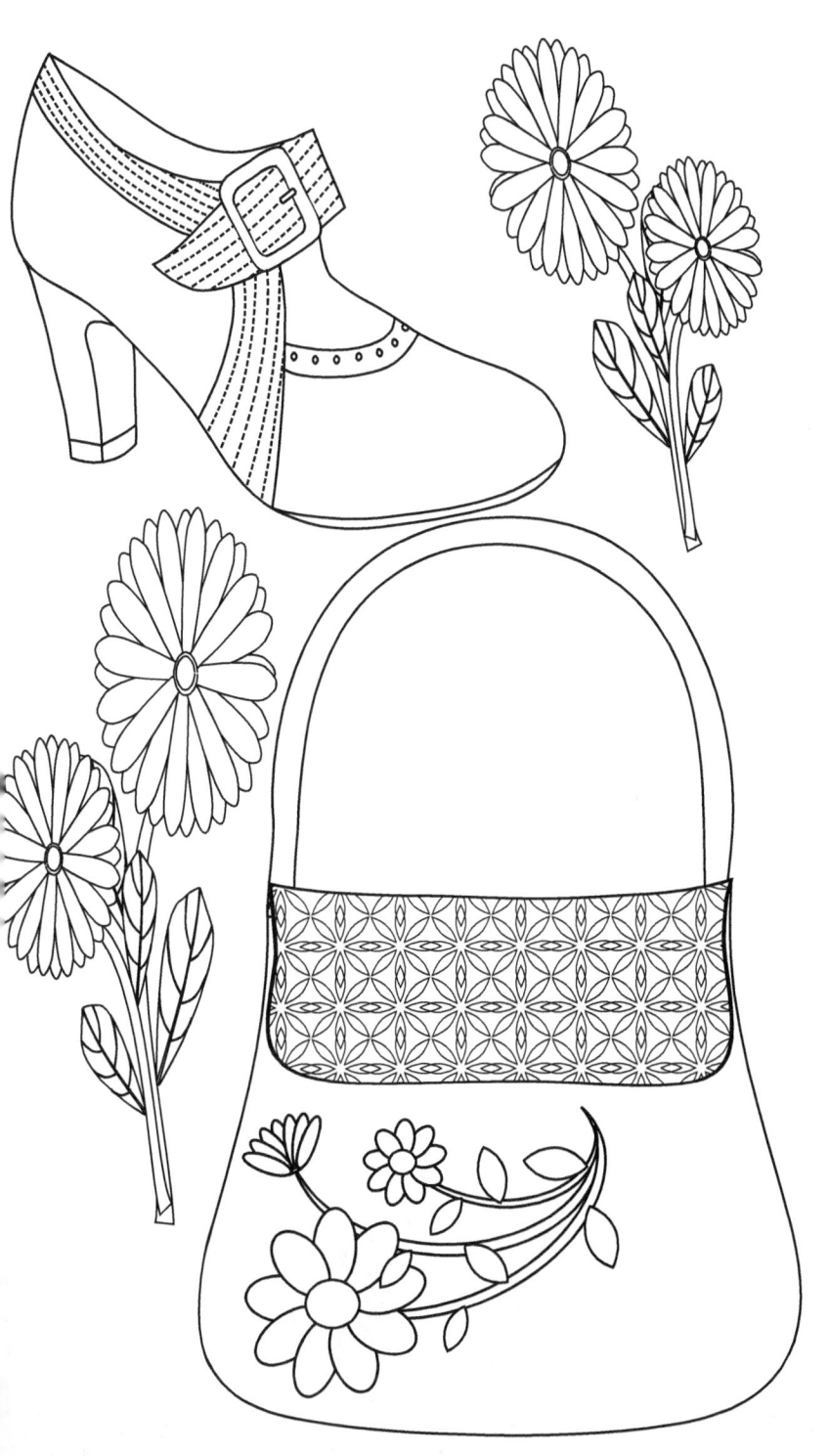

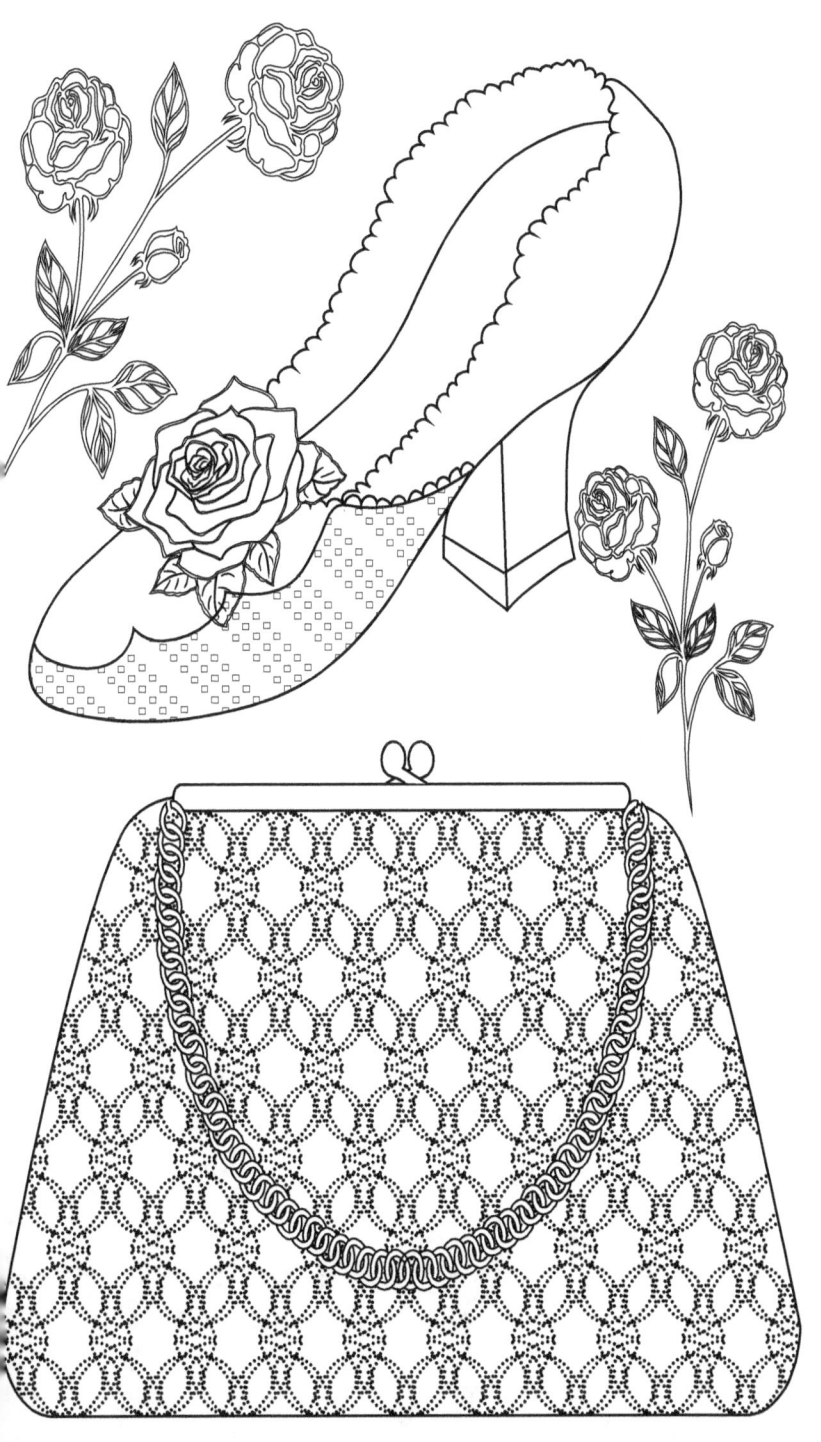

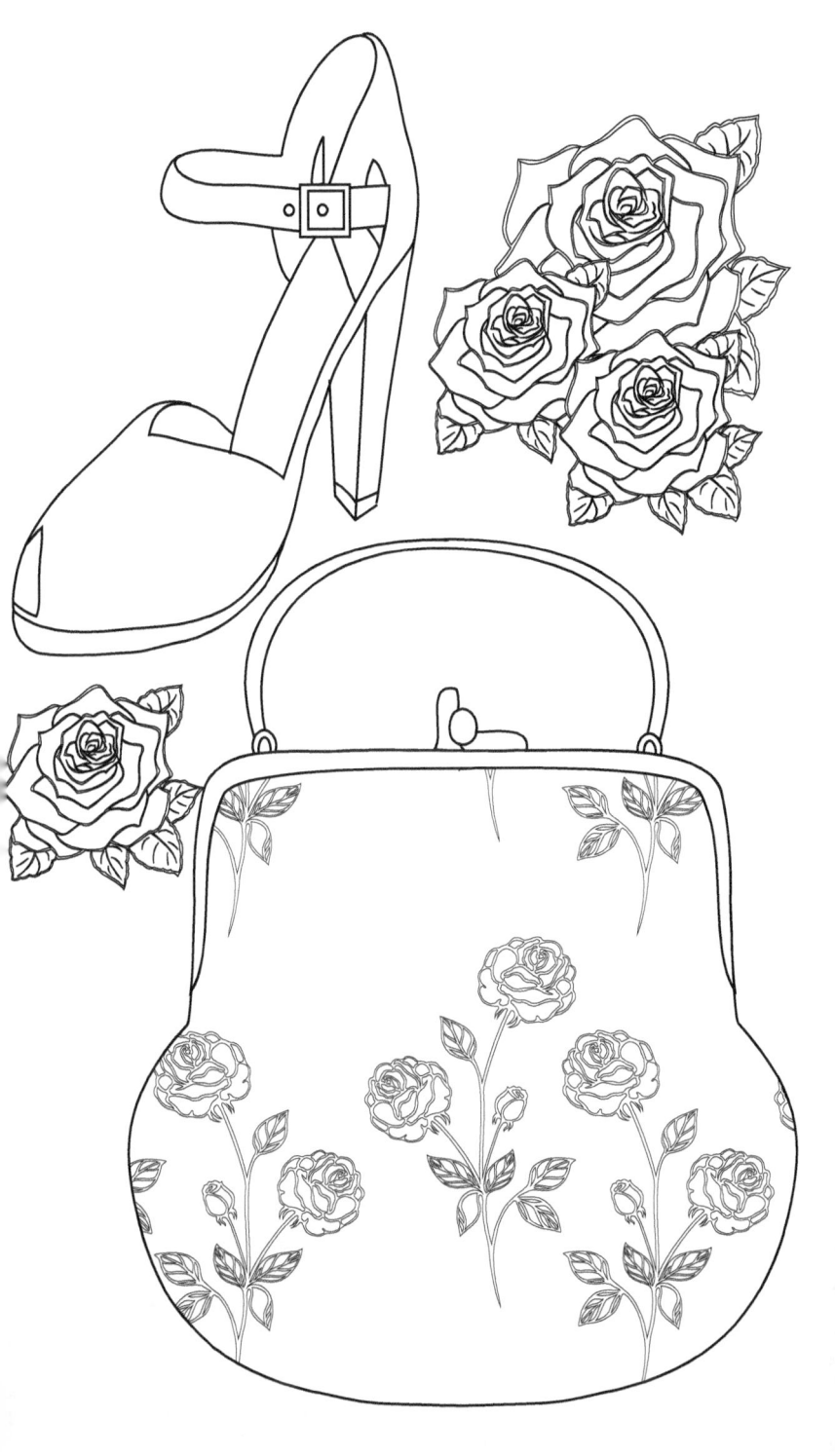

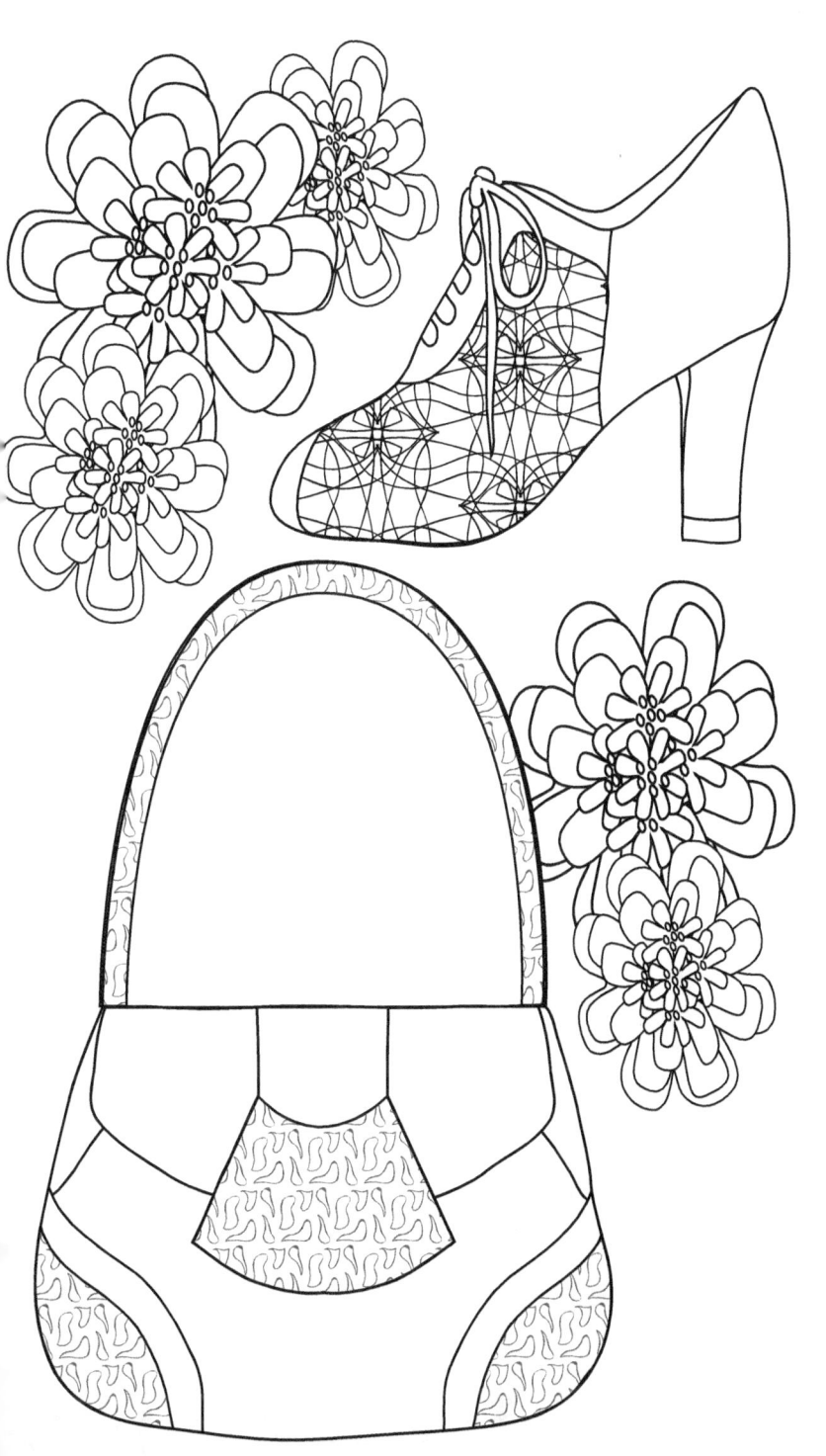

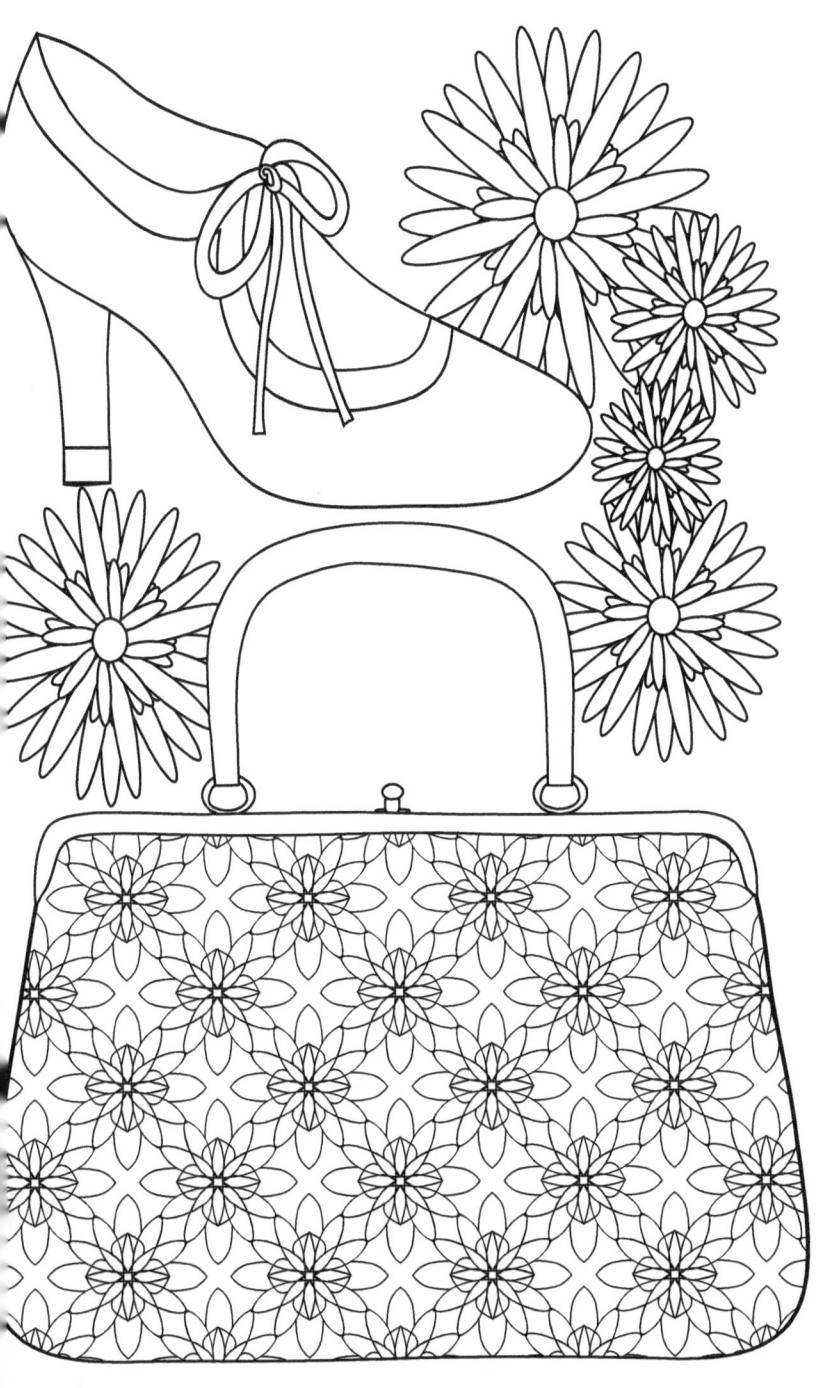

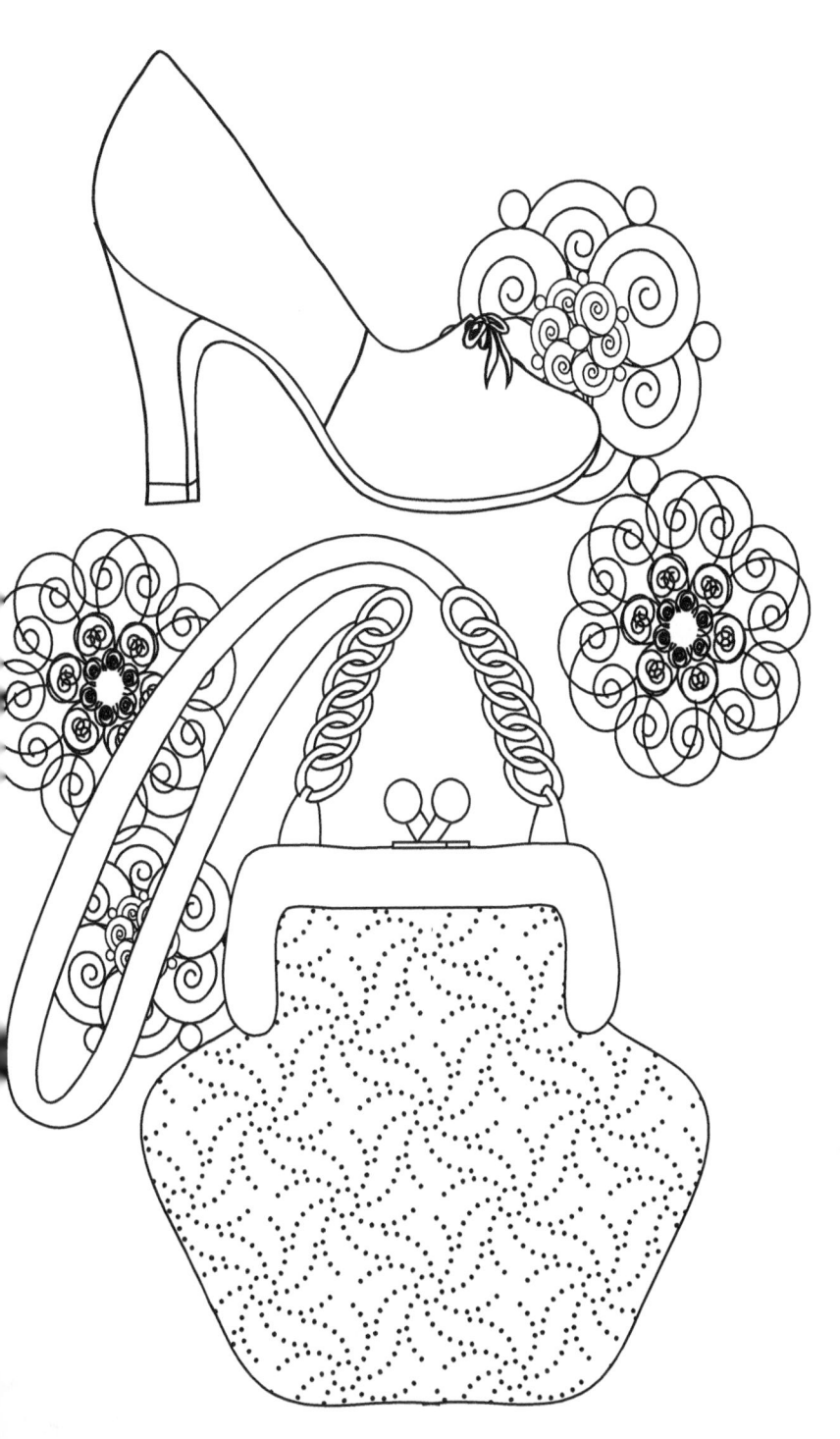

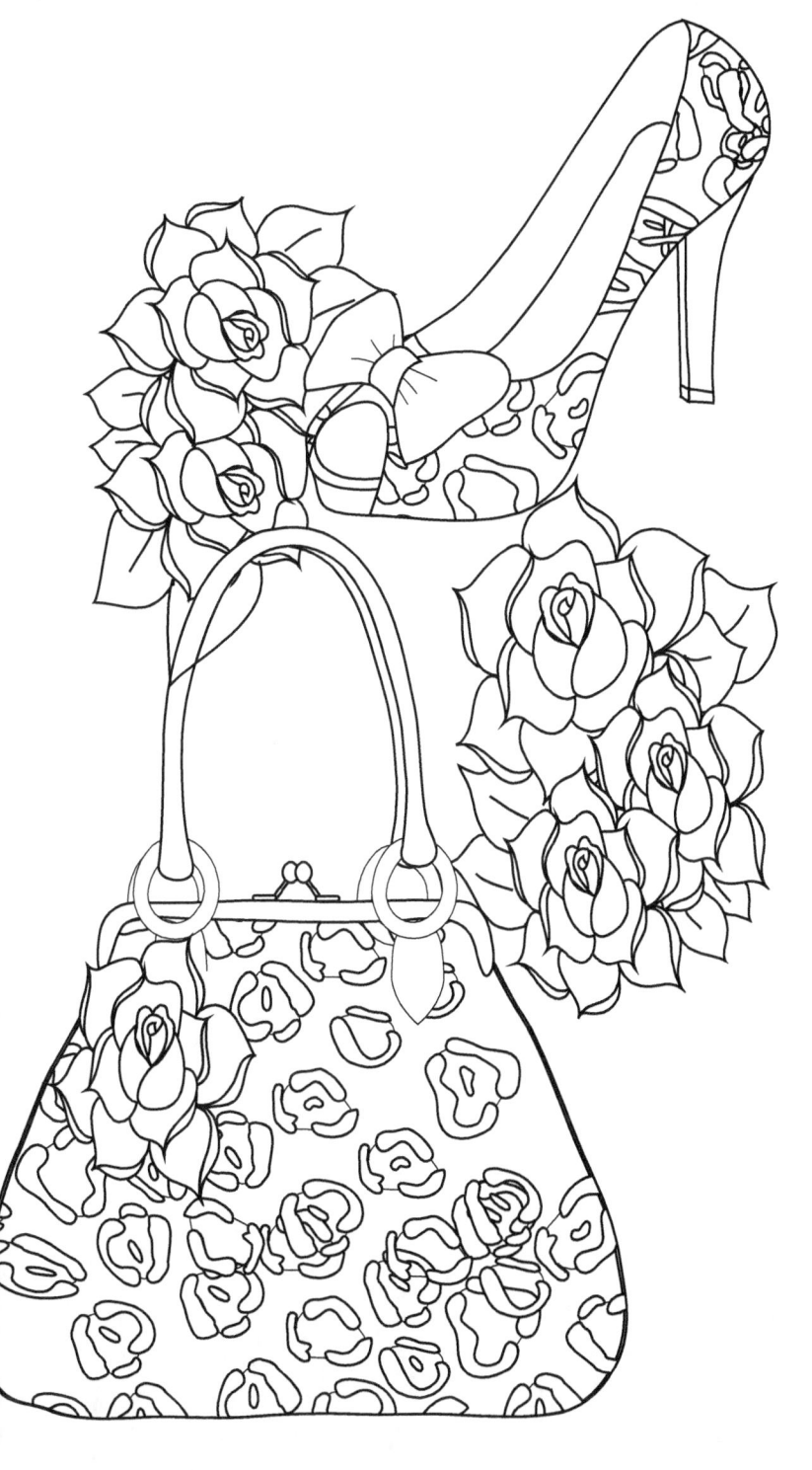

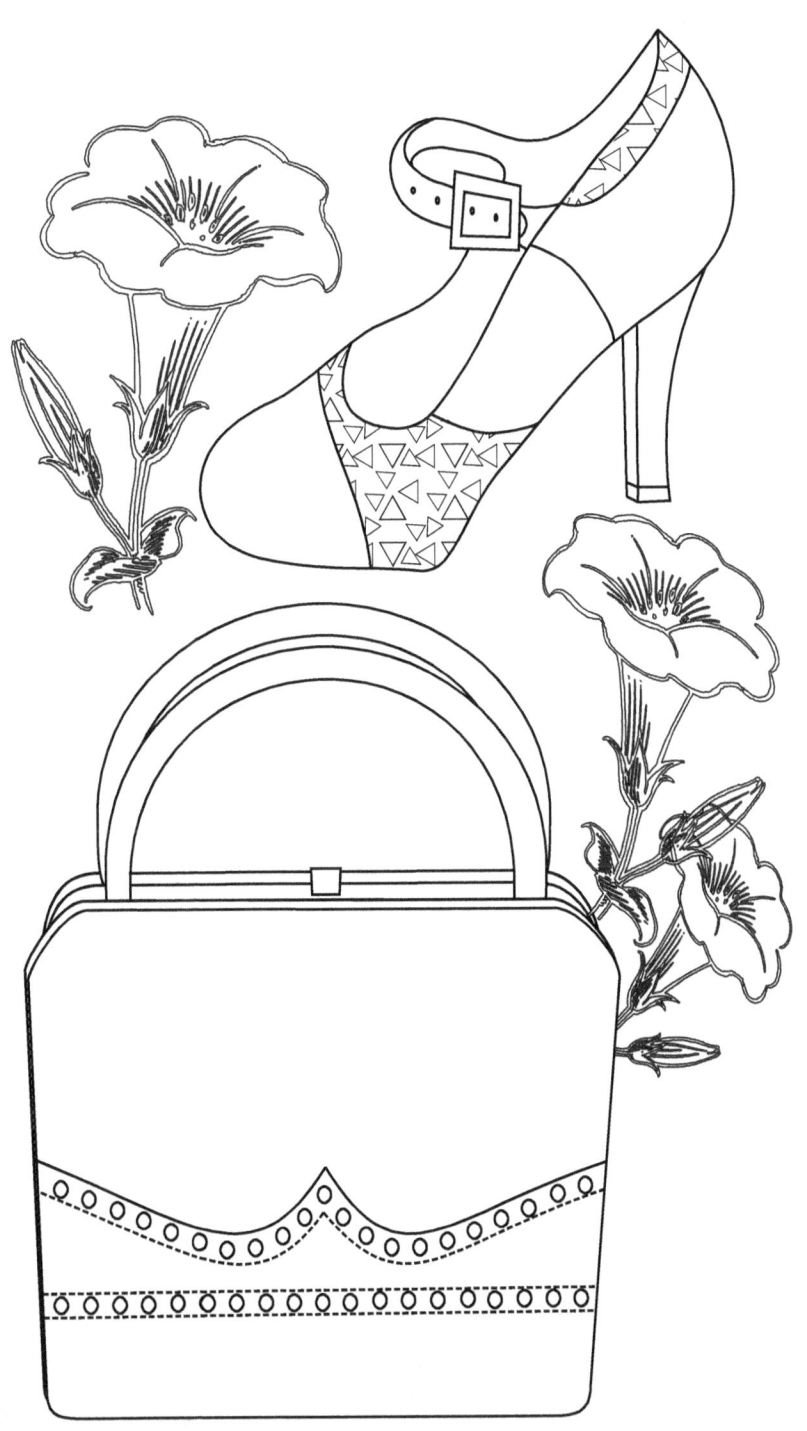

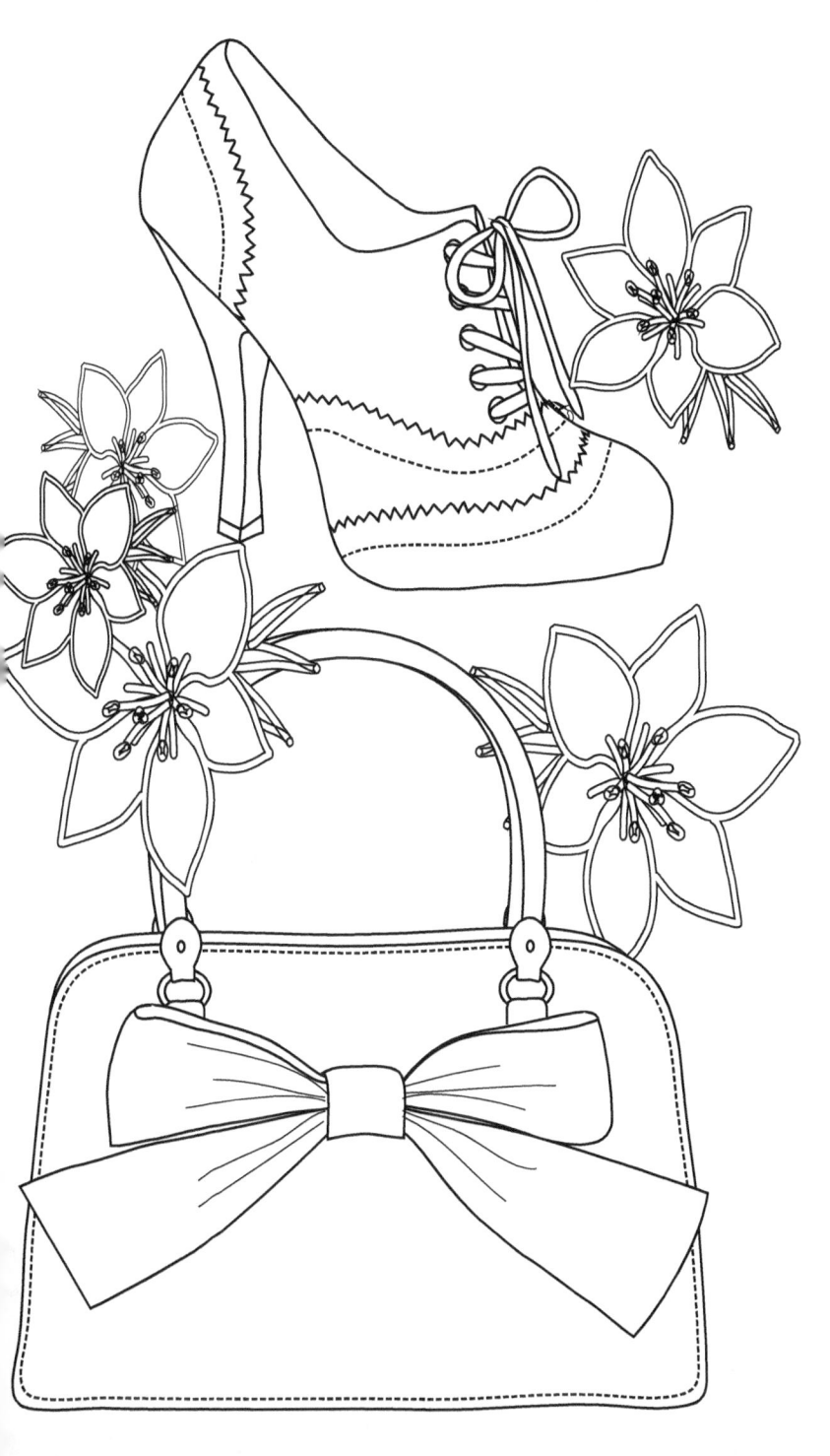

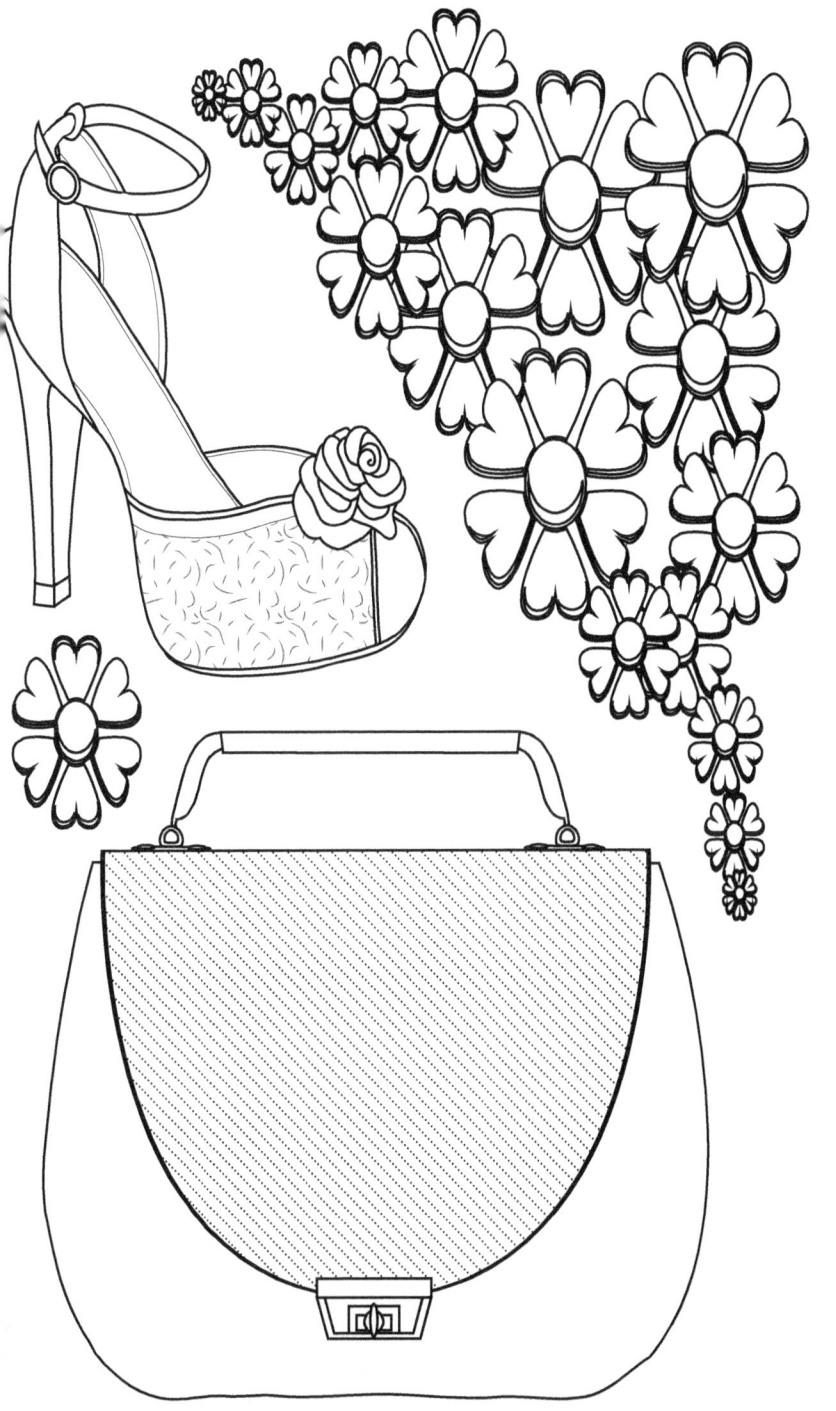

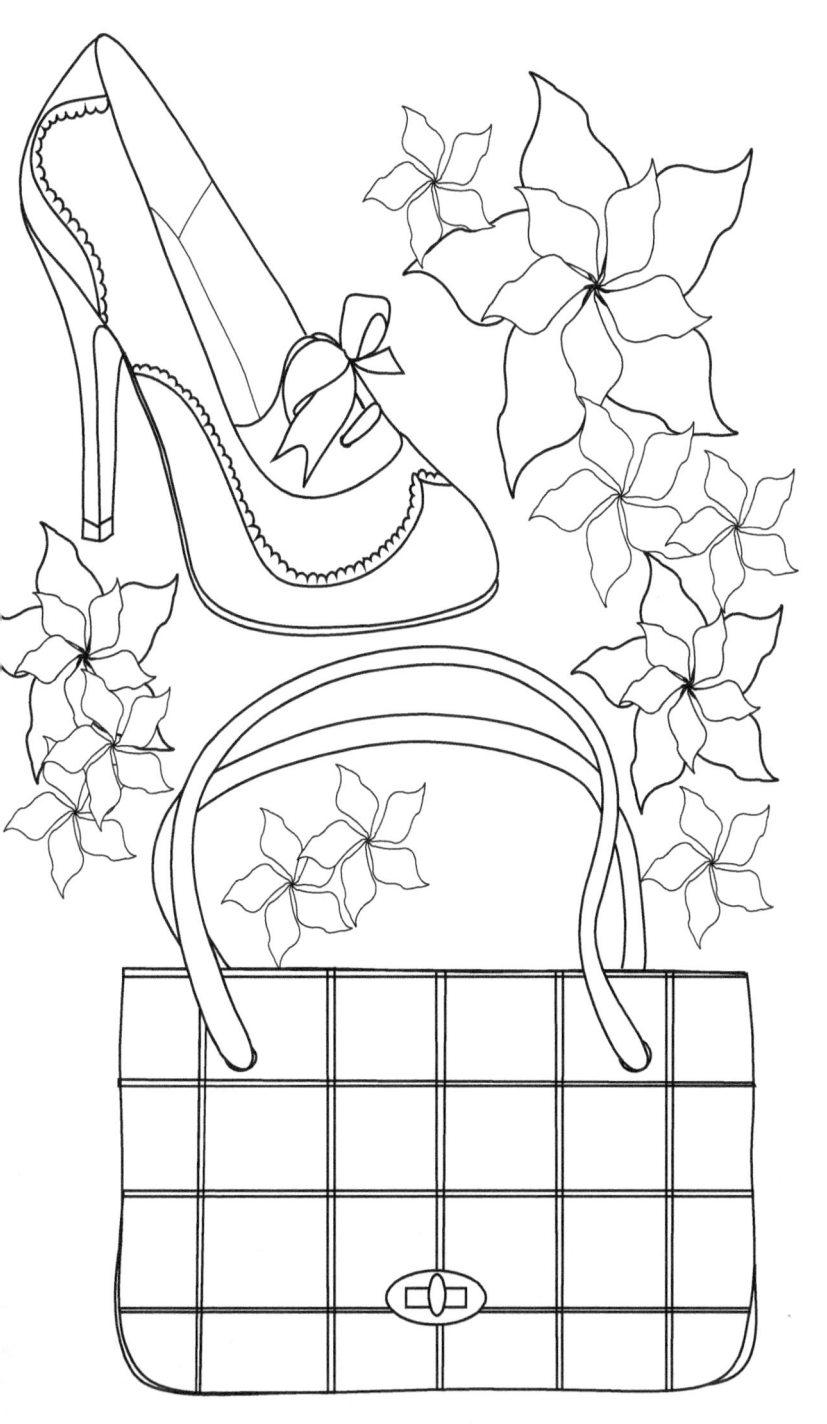

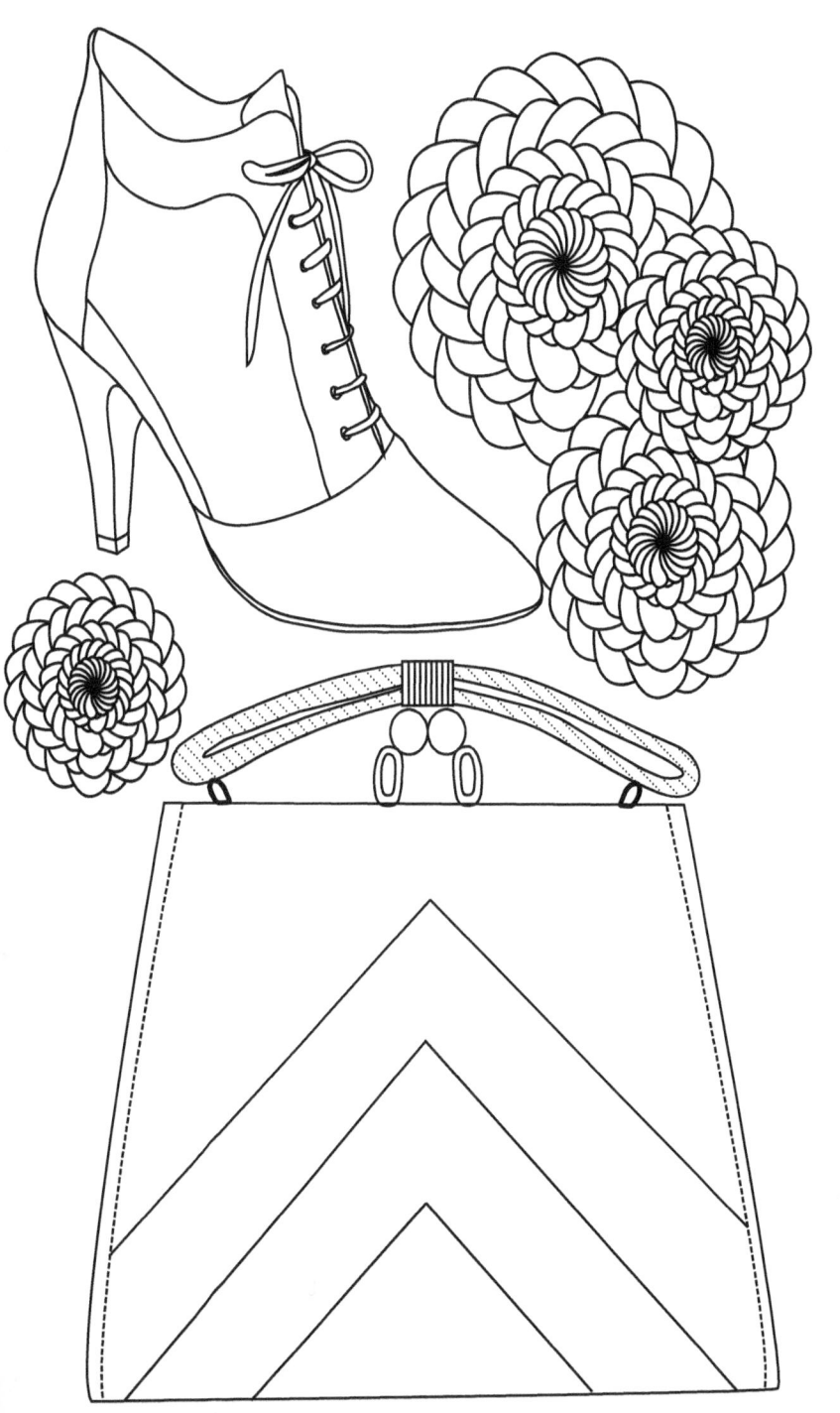

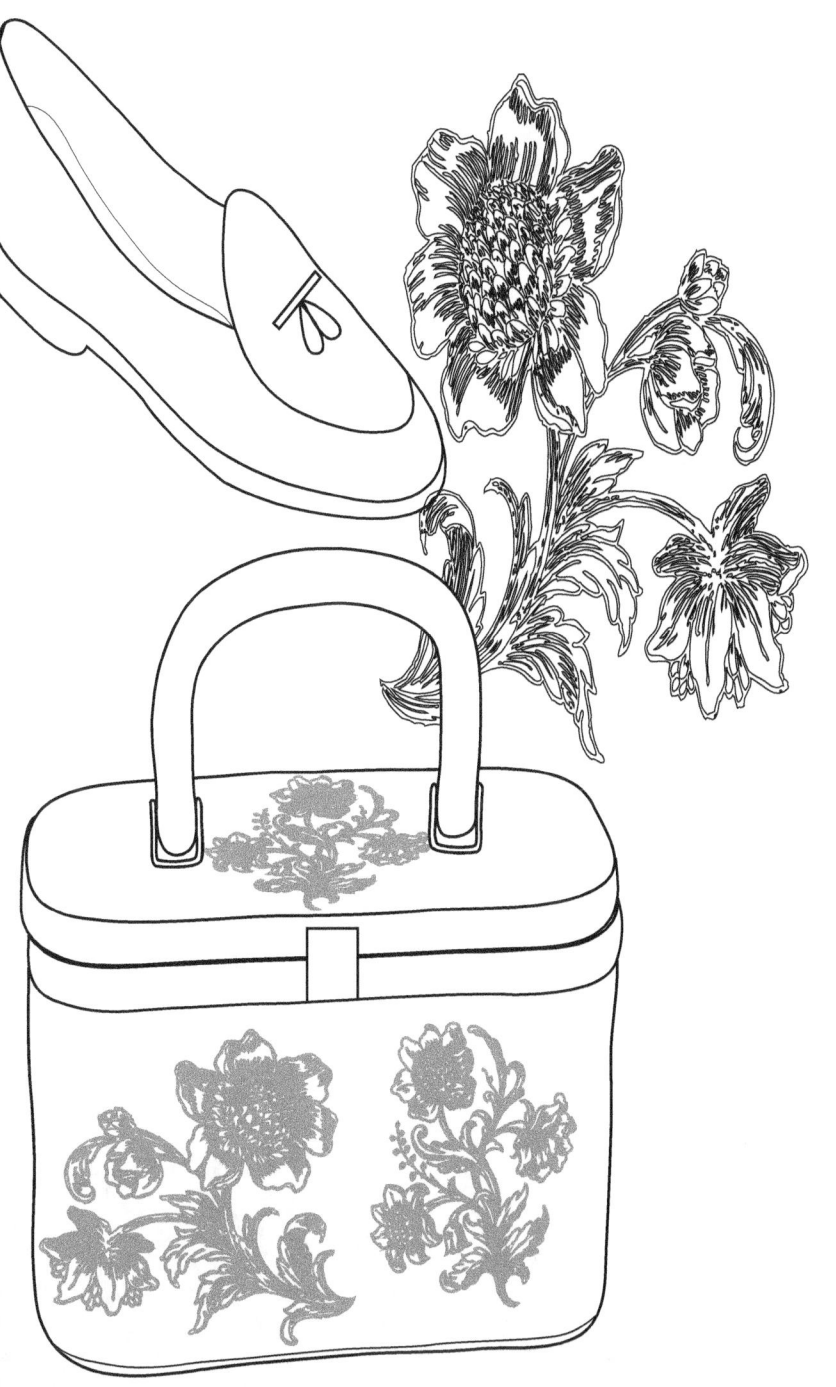

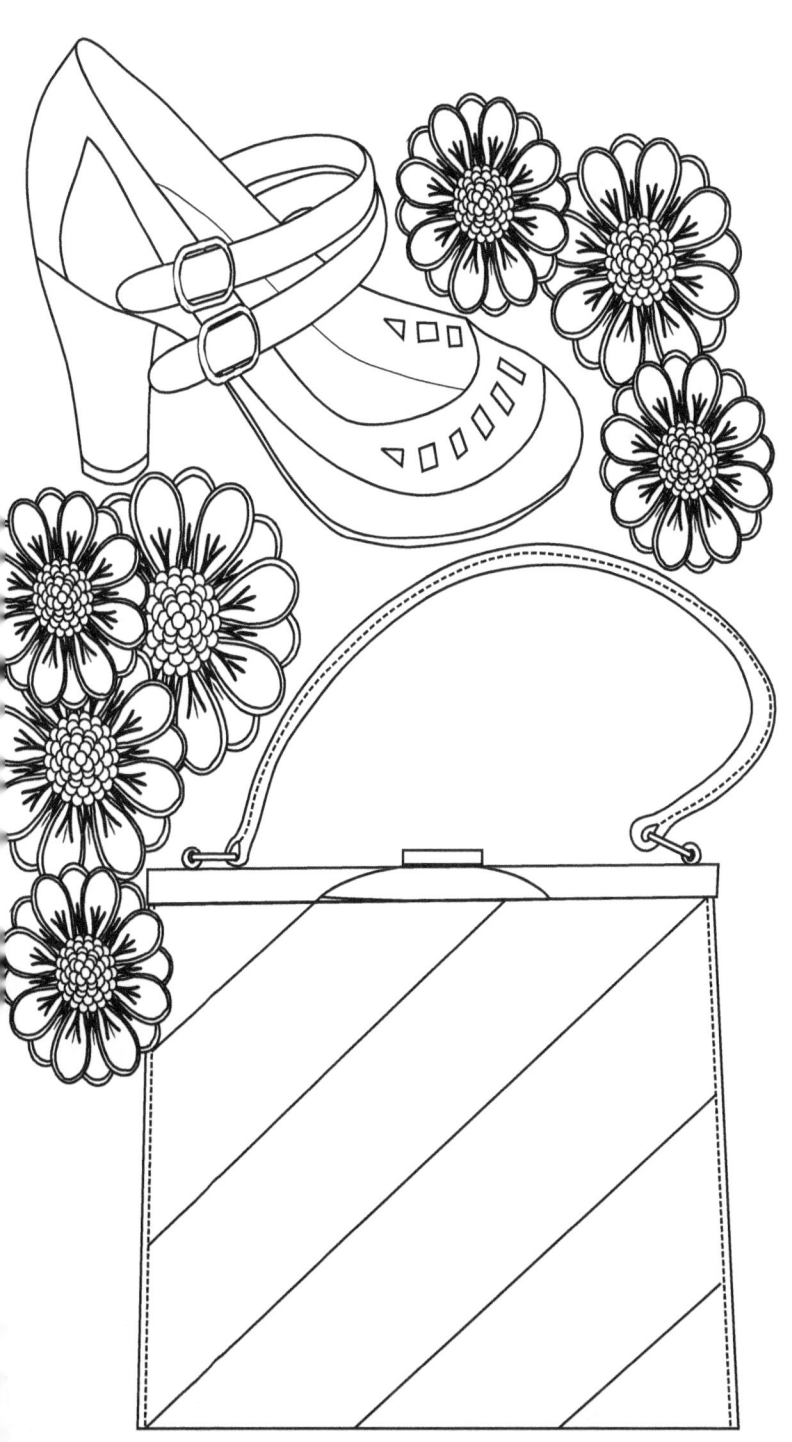

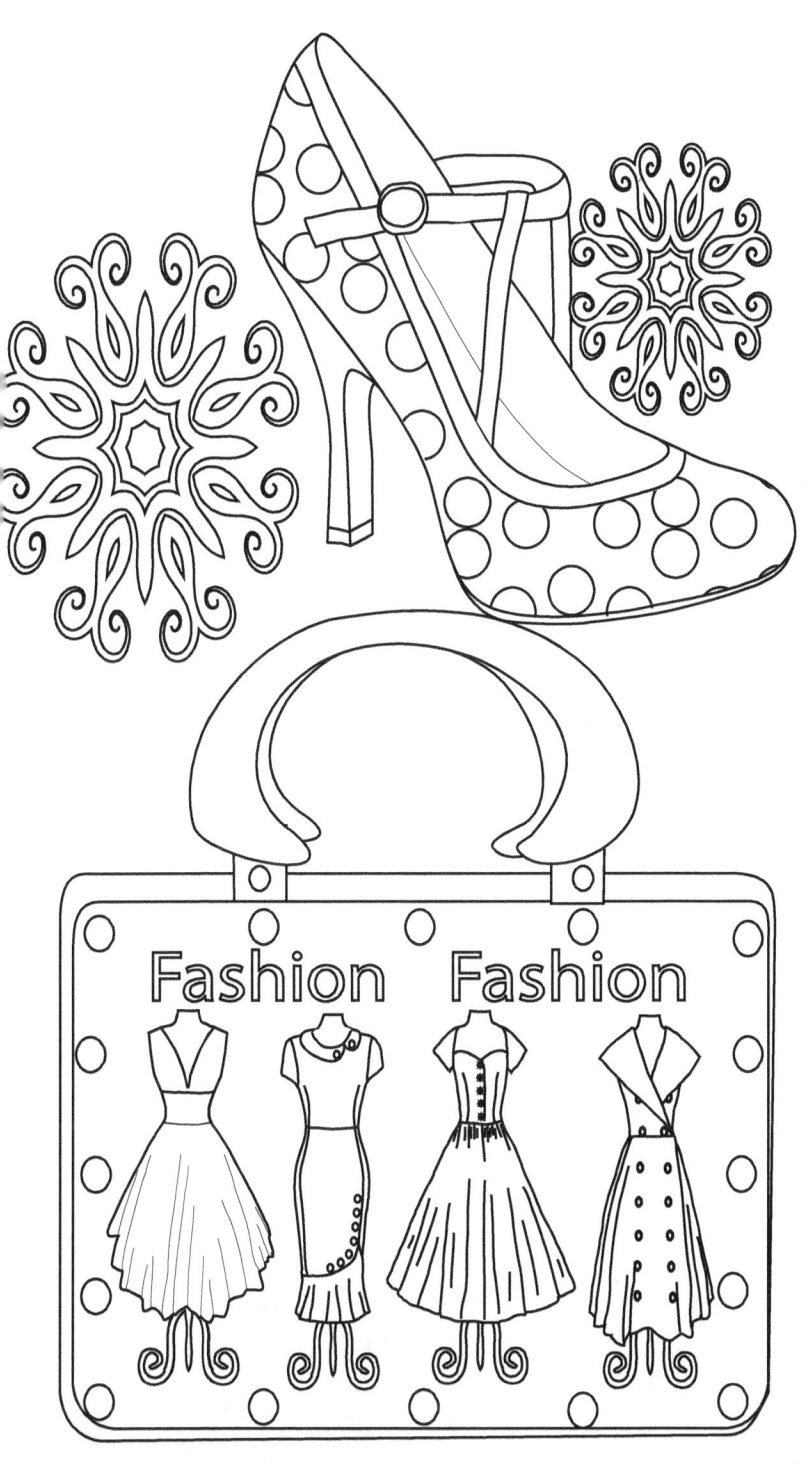

Fashion Fashion

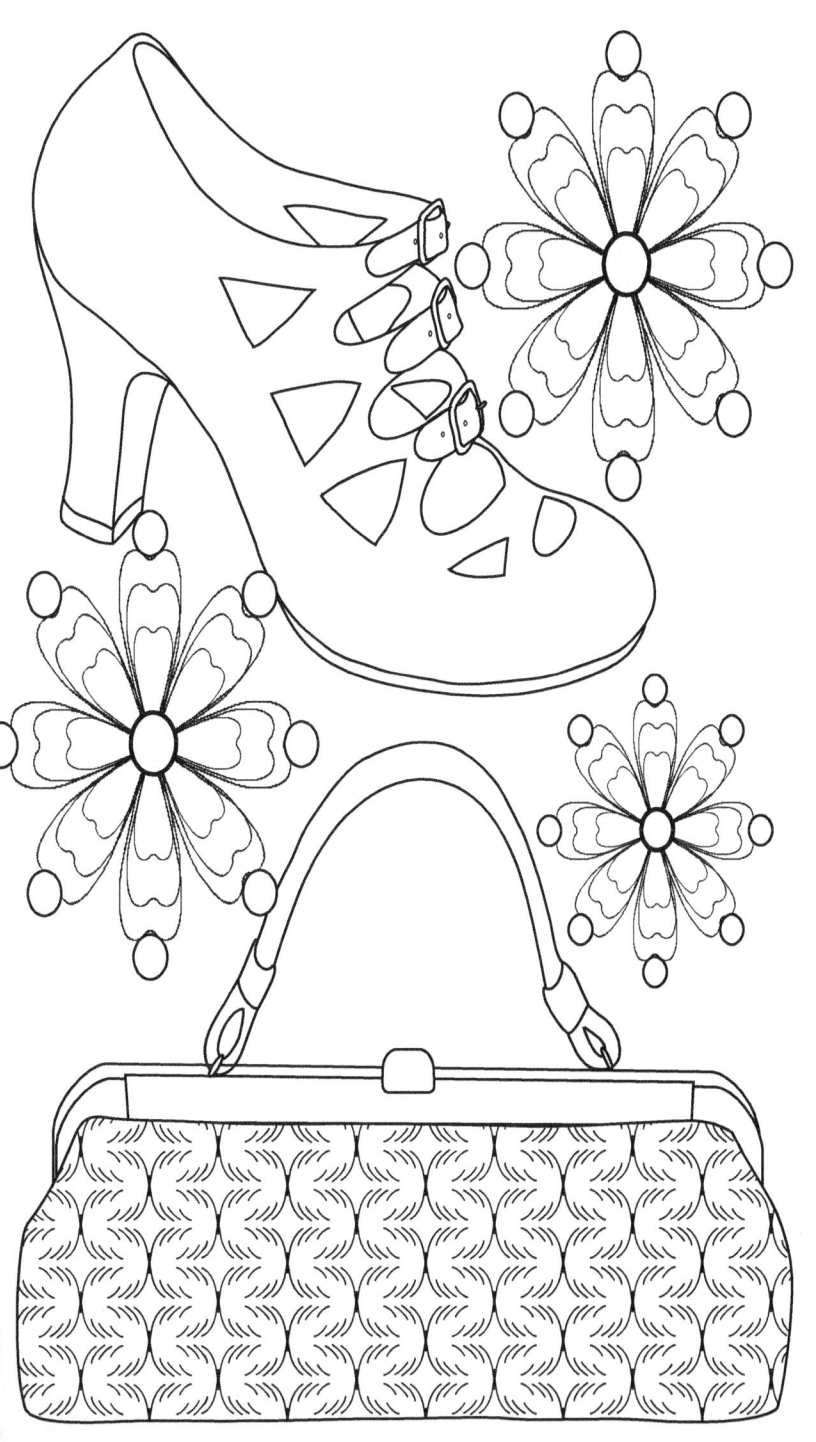

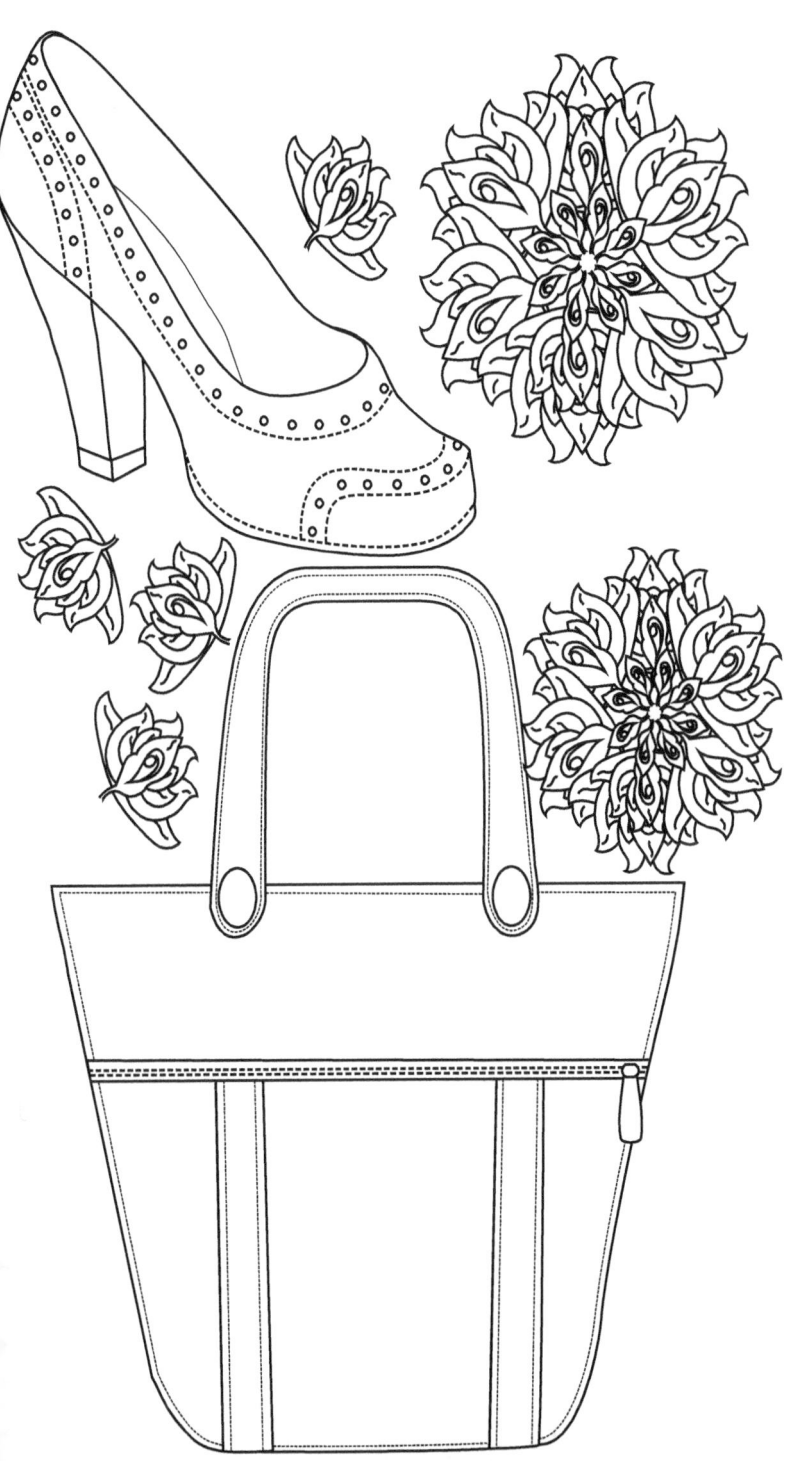

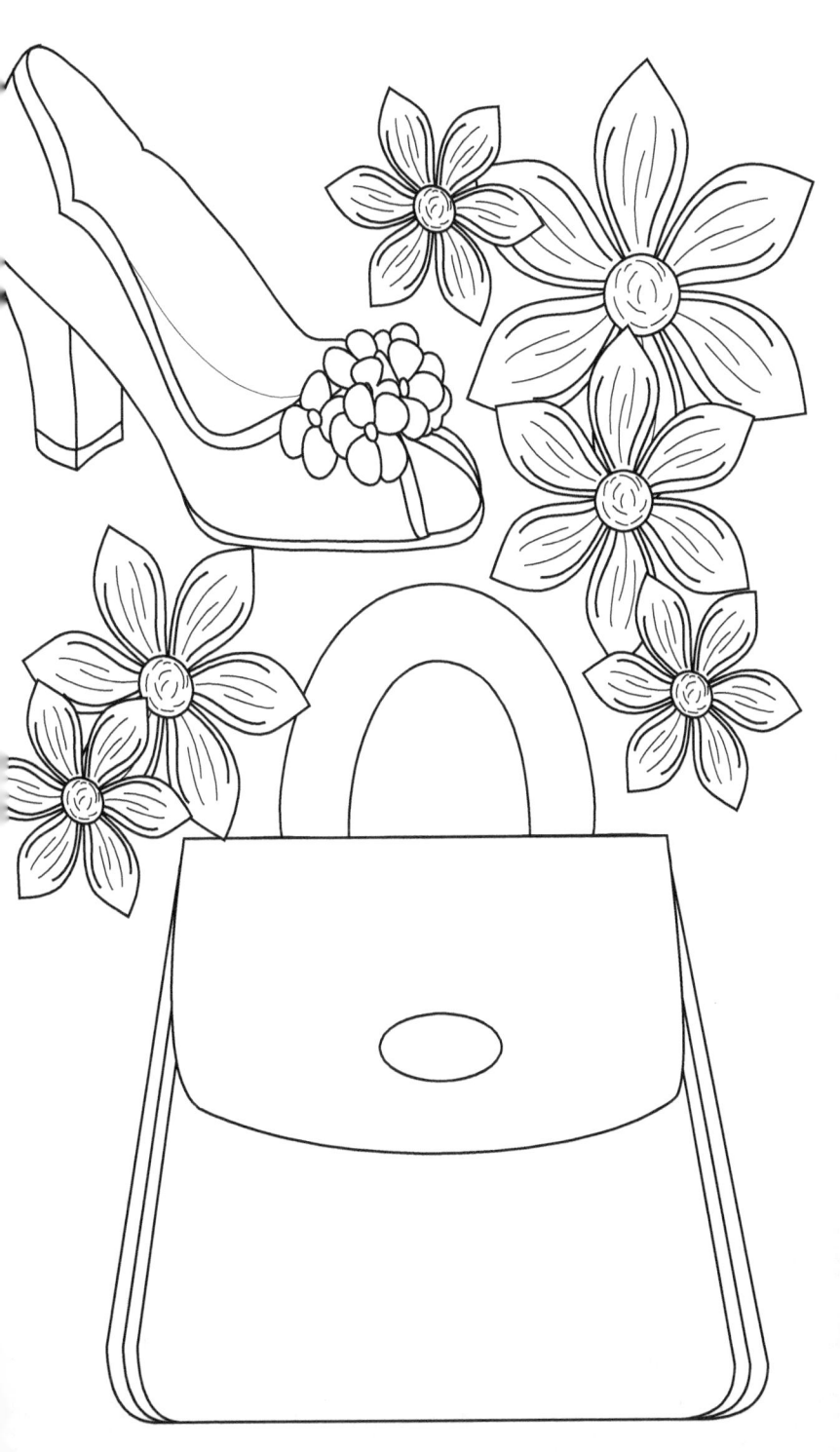

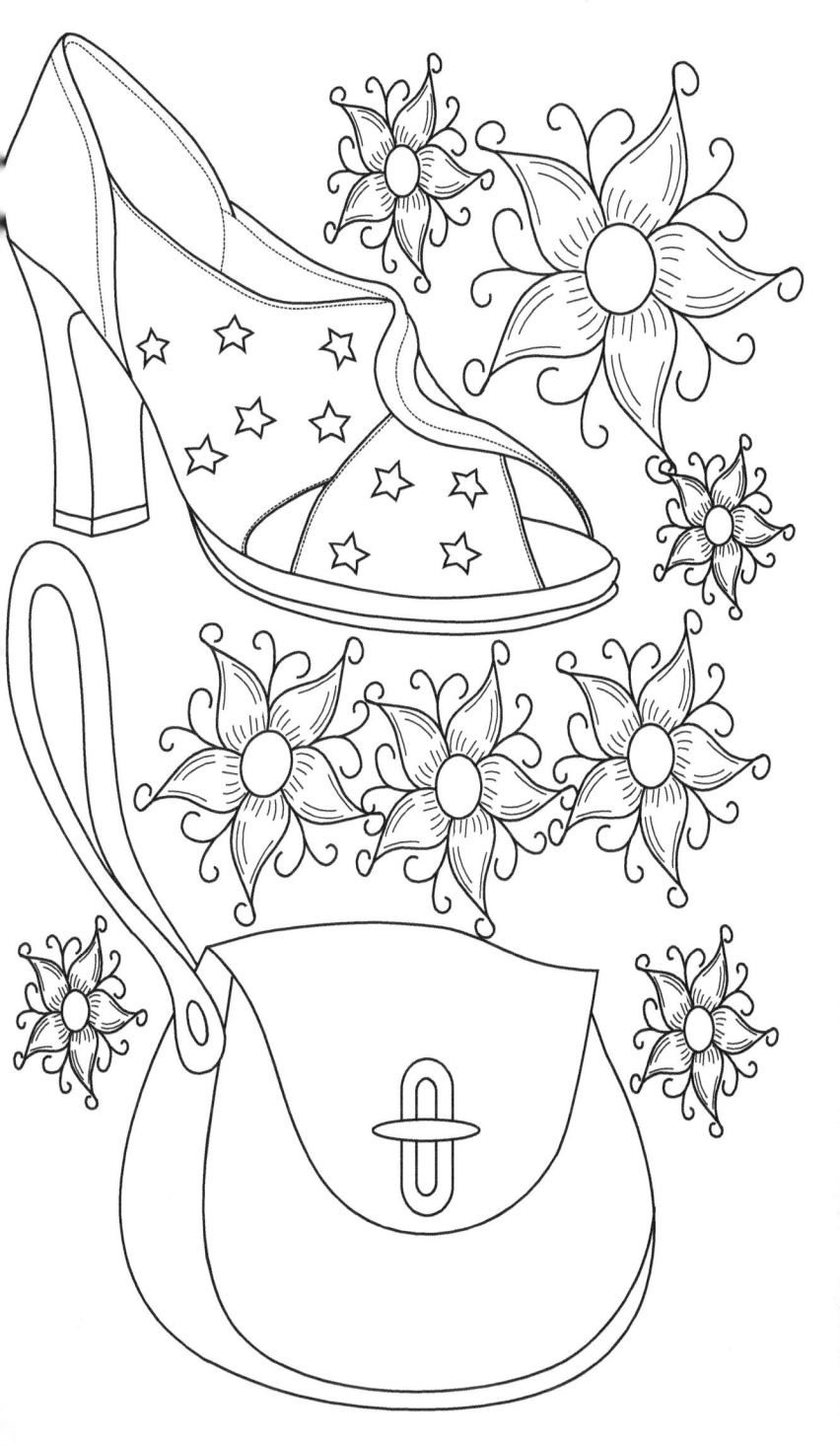

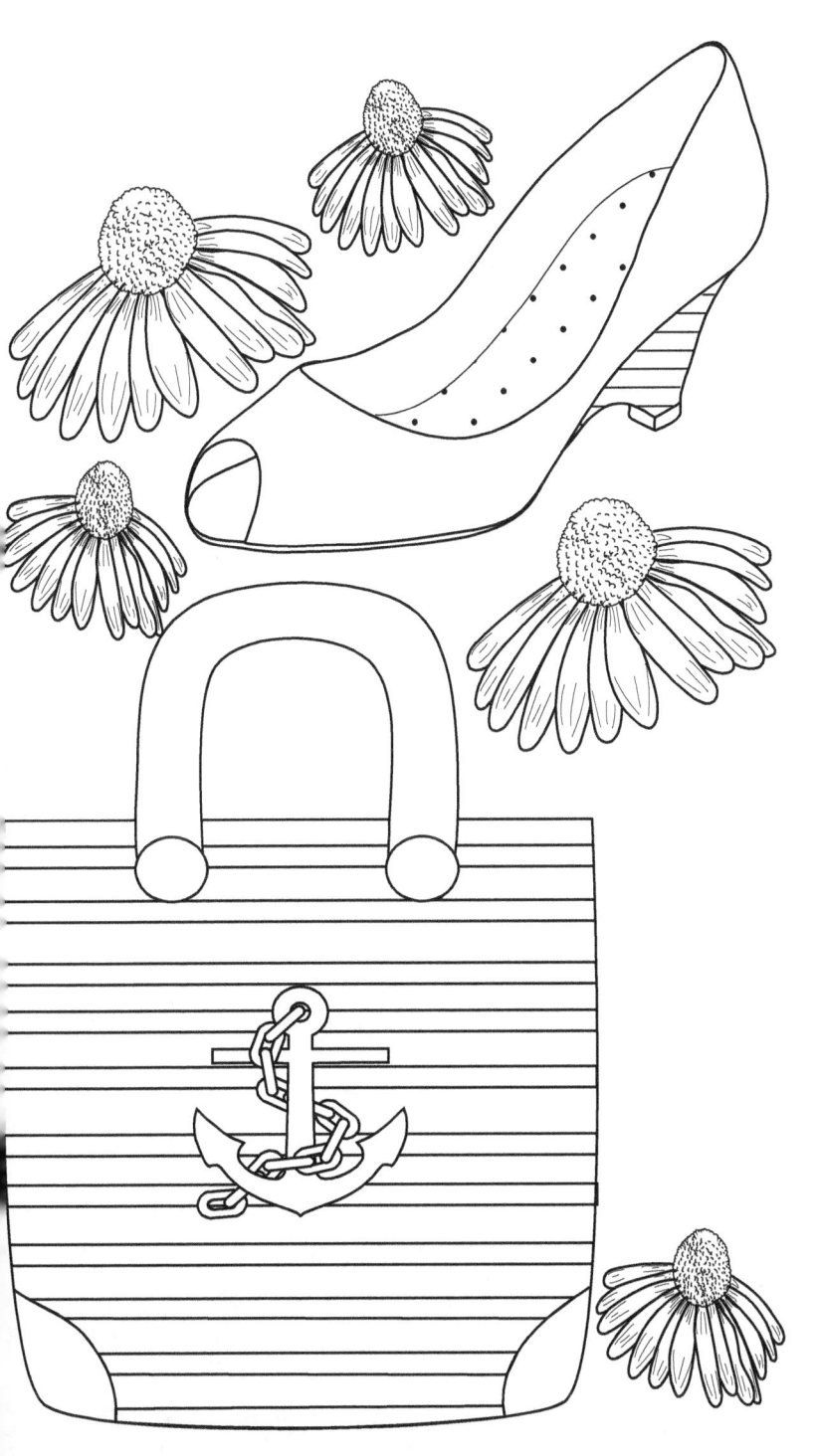

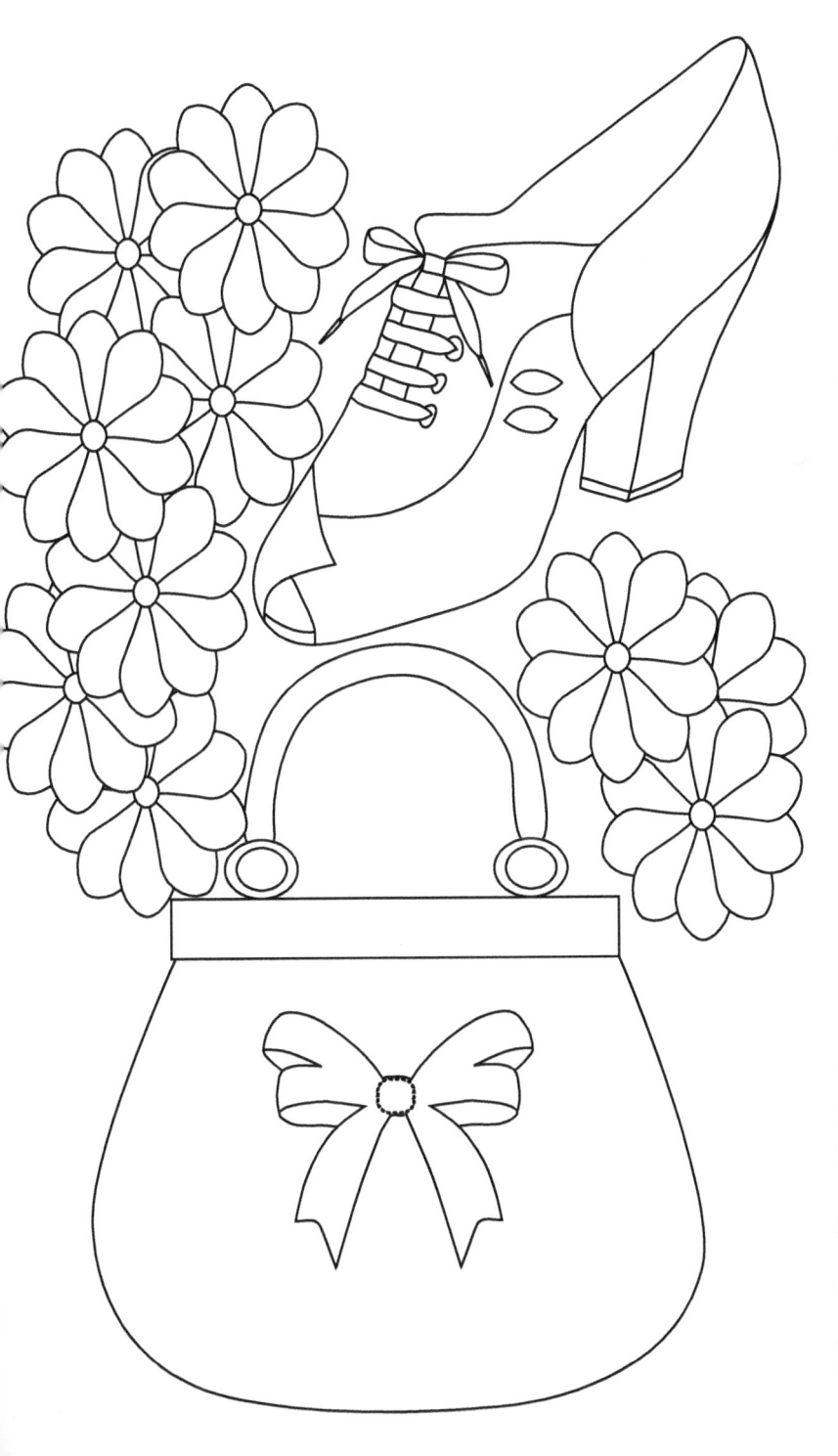

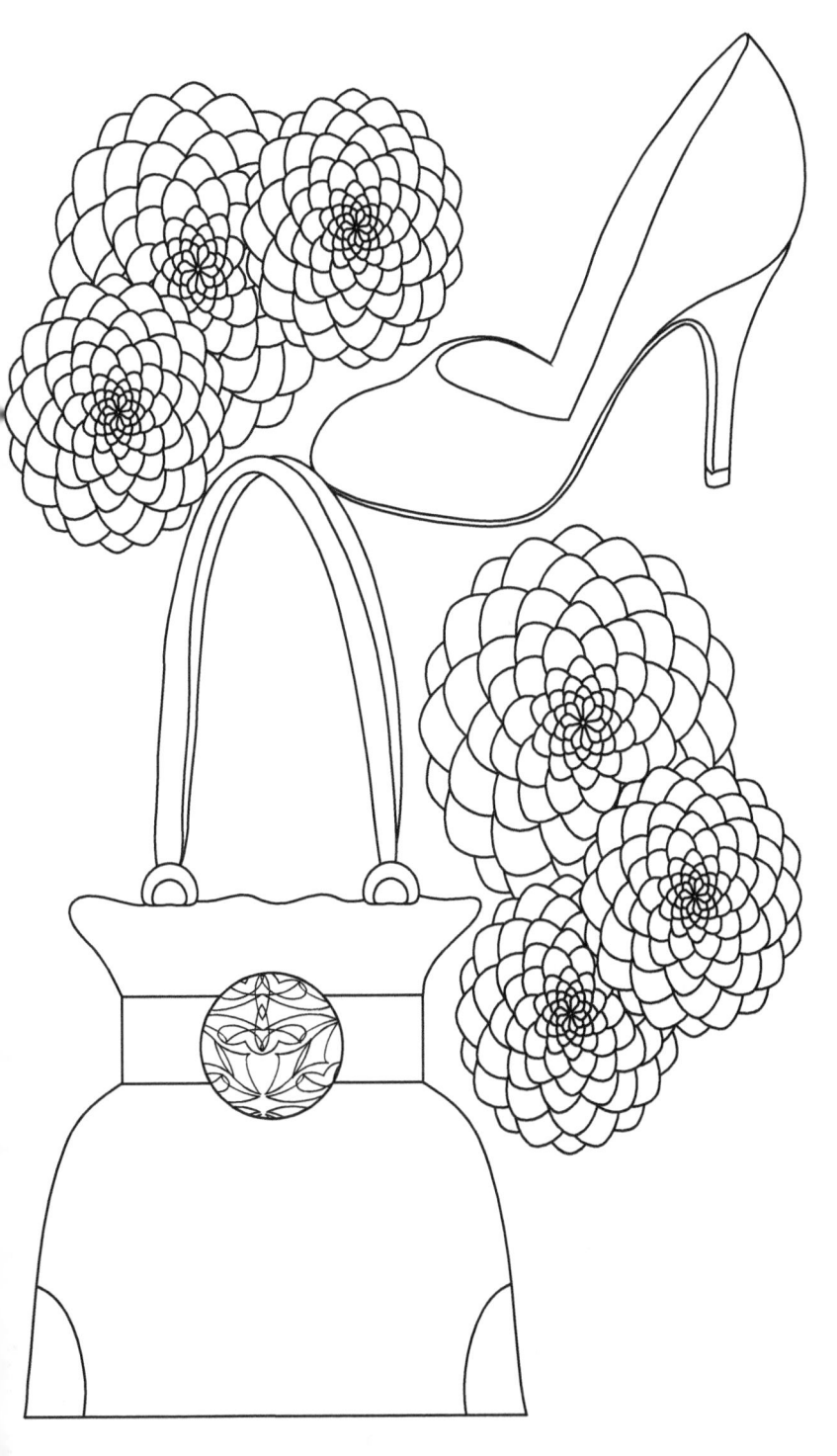

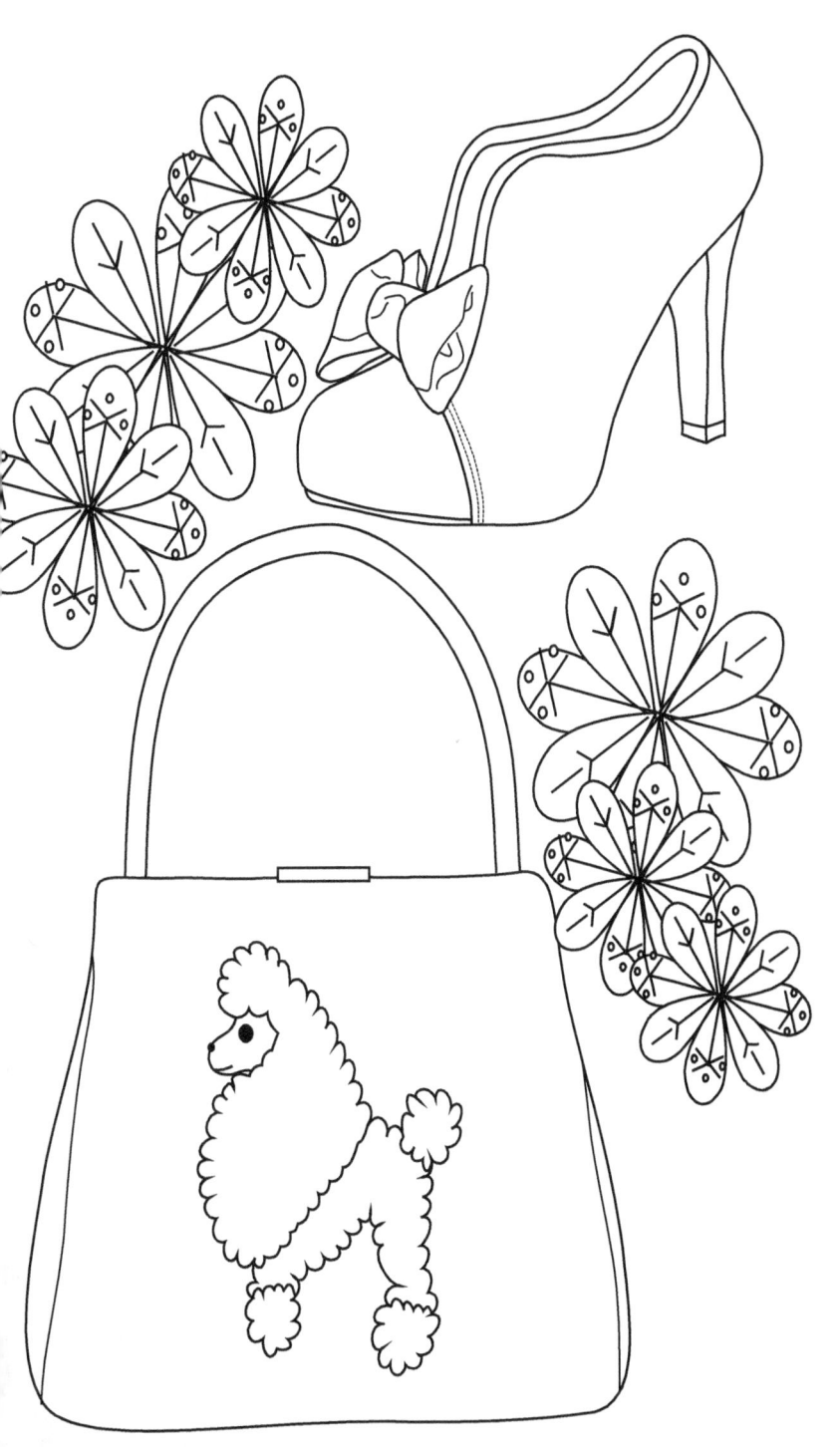

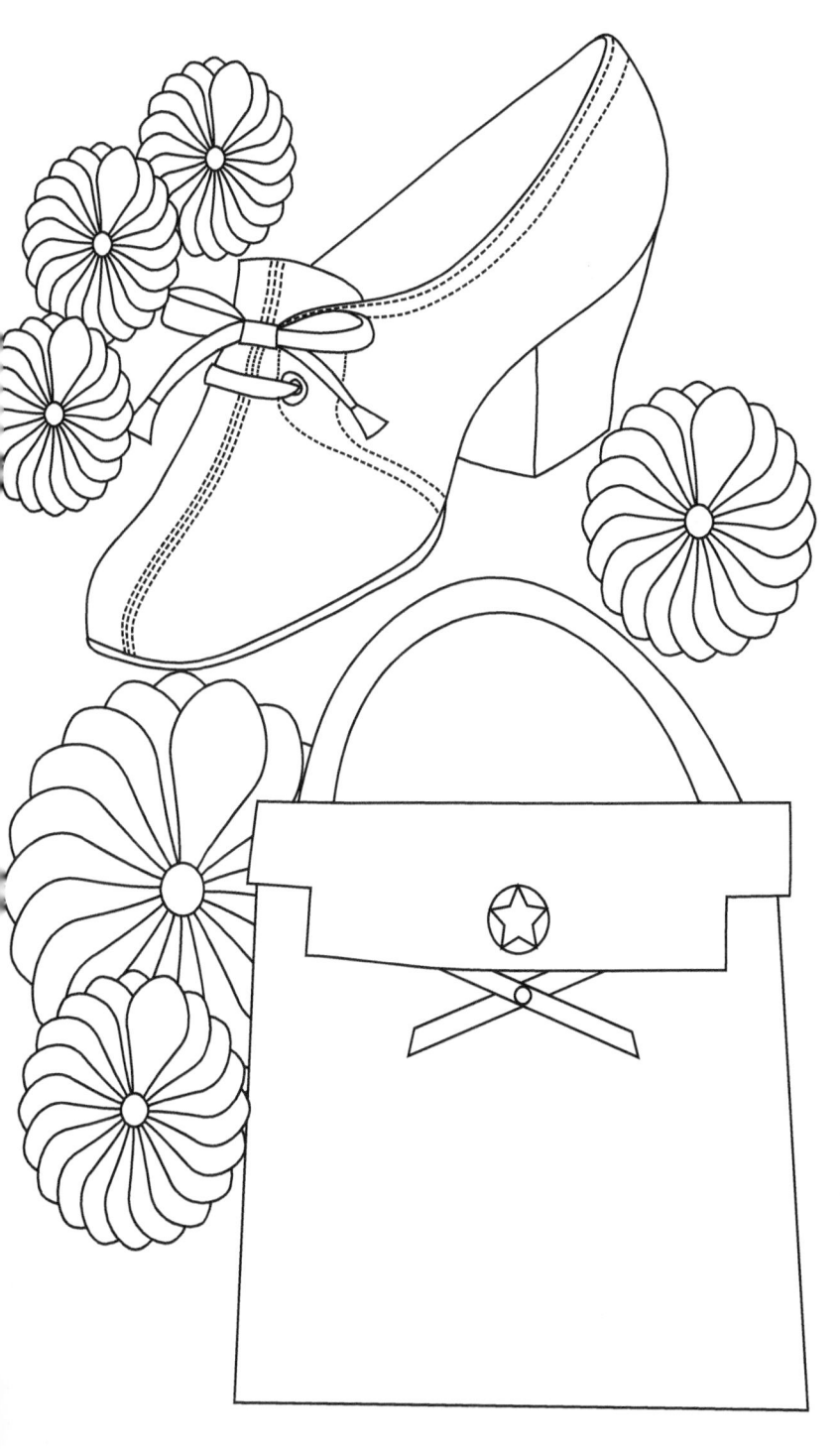

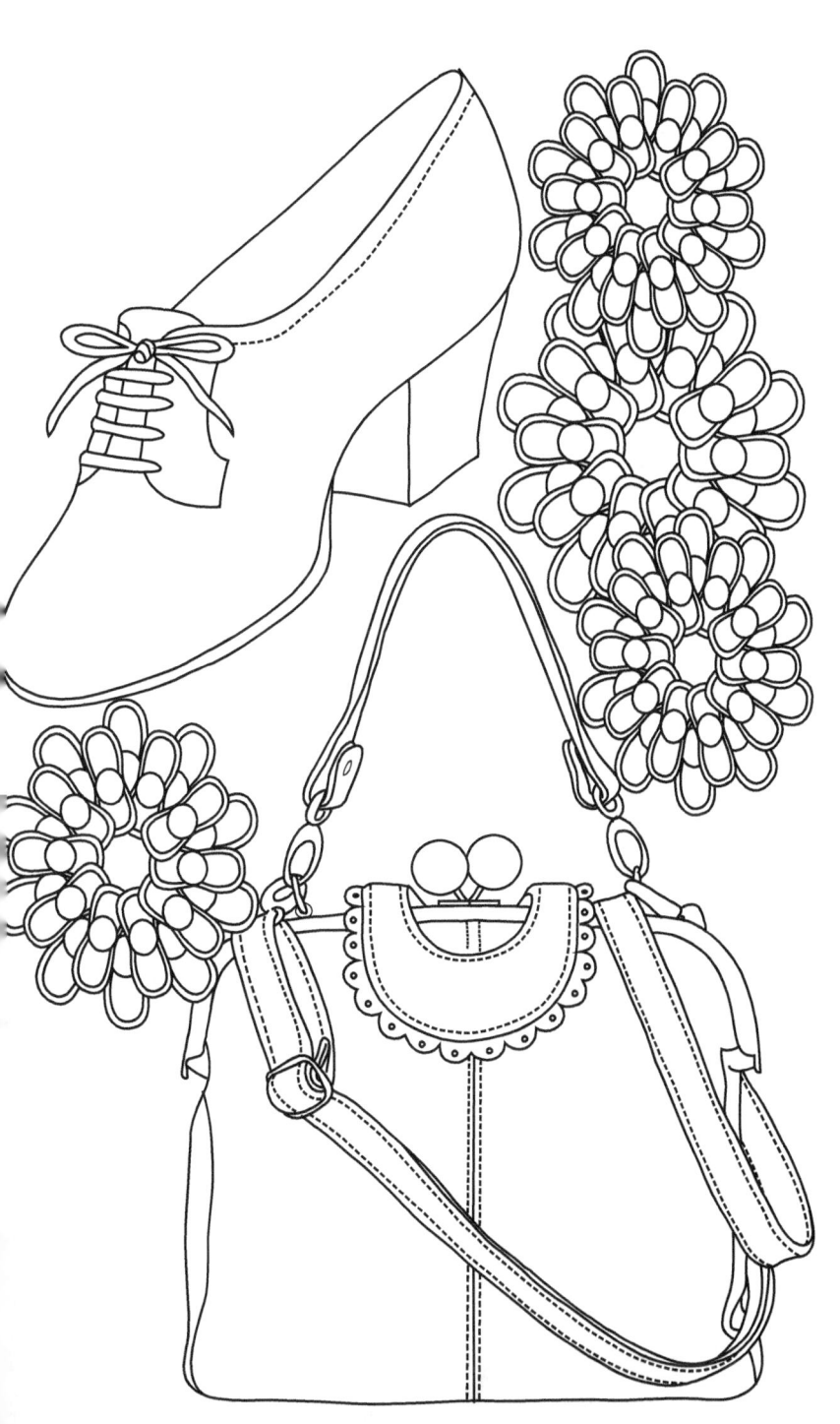

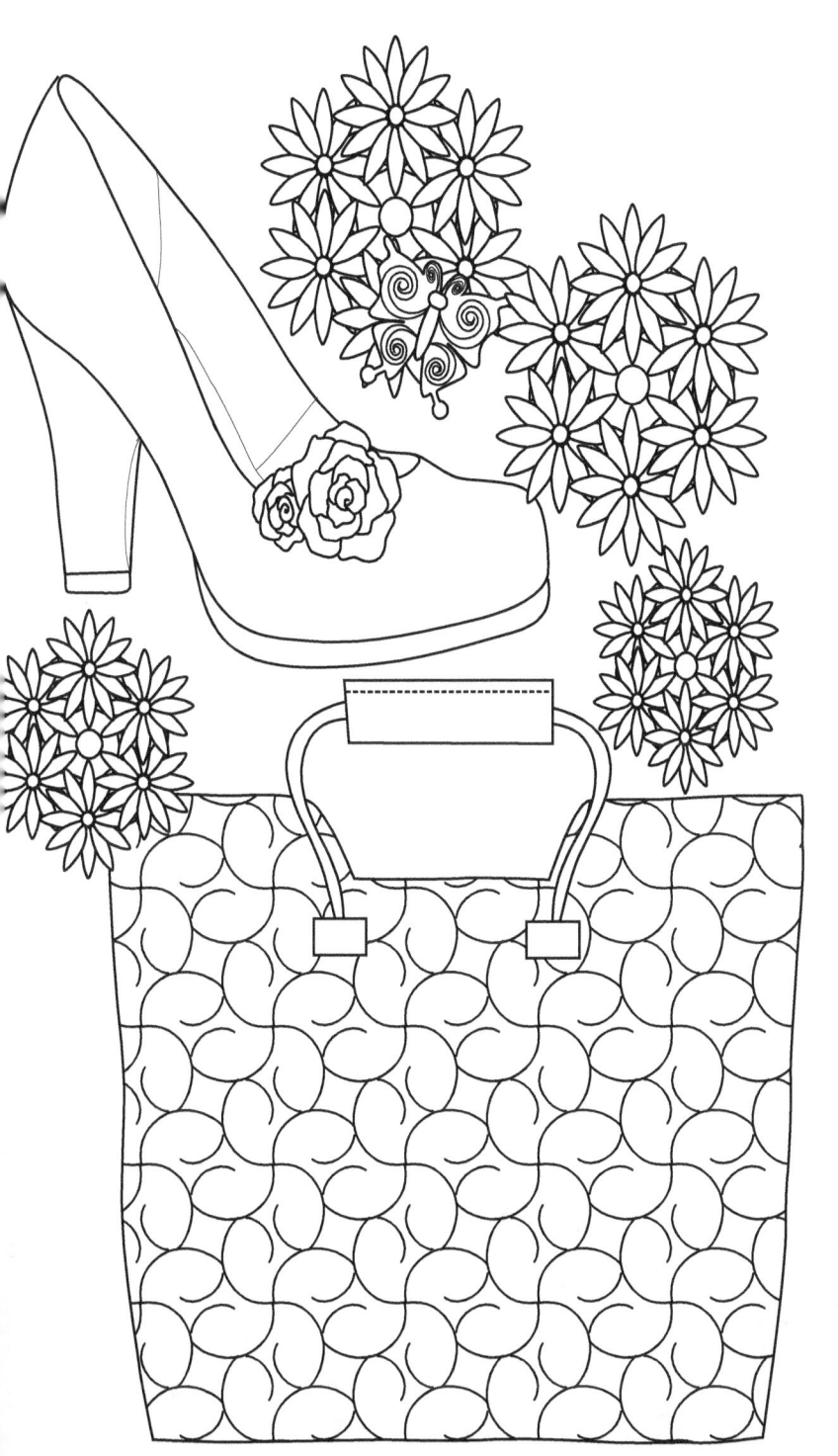

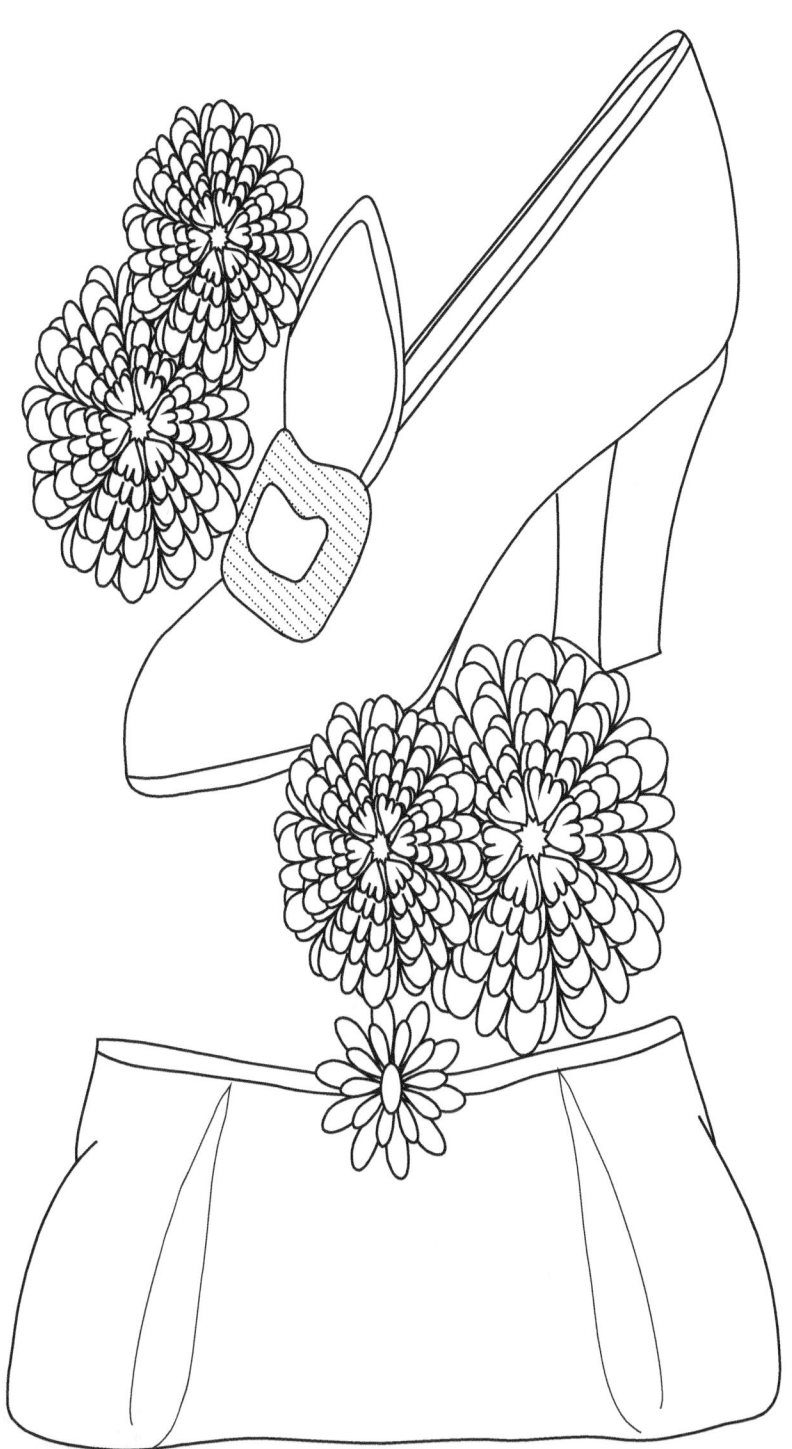

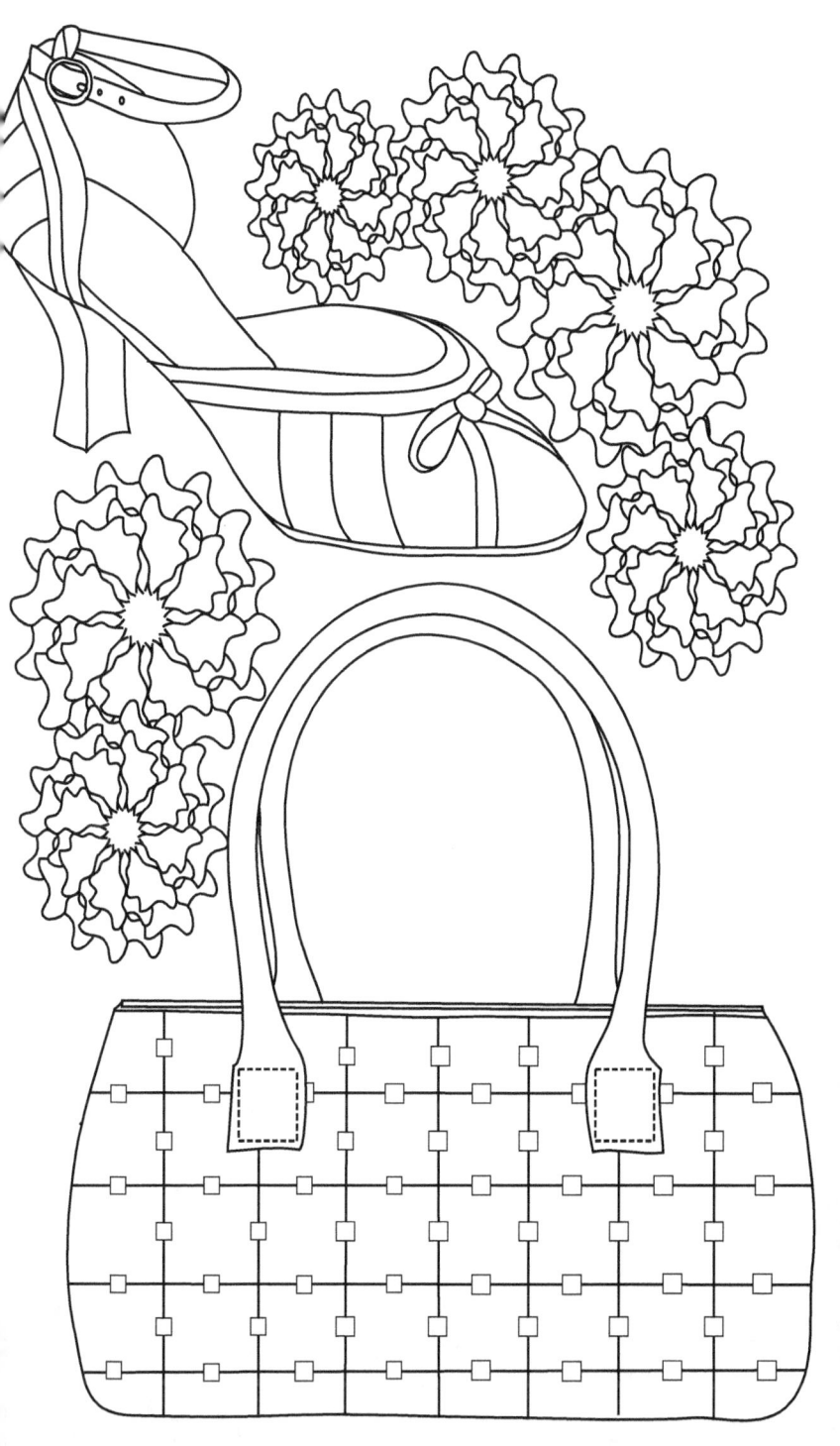

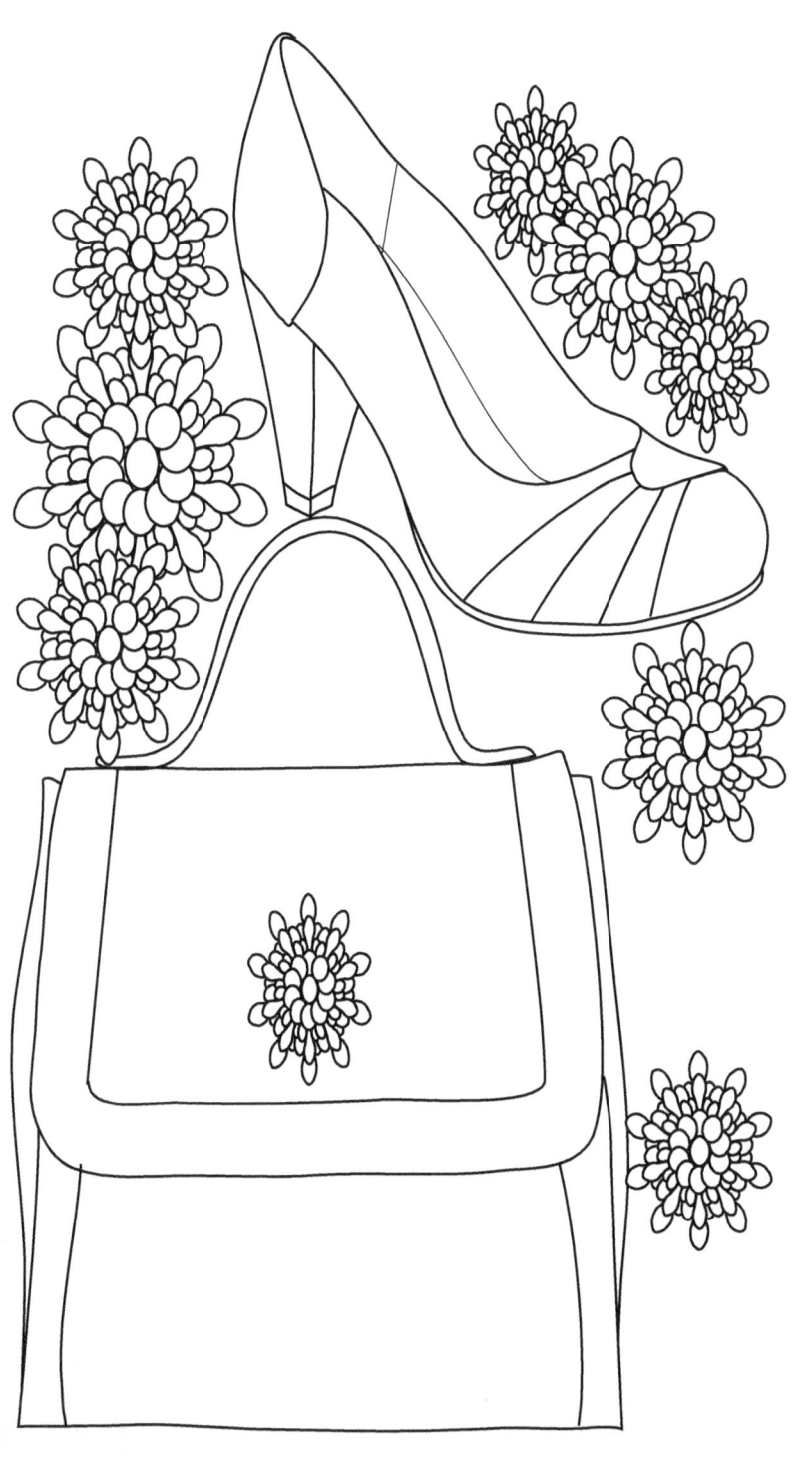

www.ingramcontent.com/pod-product-compliance
Lightning Source LLC
Chambersburg PA
CBHW070402190526
45169CB00003B/1066